Discerning Your Season

Where are you? What is your purpose?
What should you be doing <u>right</u> <u>now</u>!?

Anya Miller Hall

Dedication

This book is dedicated to my parents, **Benjamin F.** and **Myrtle C. Miller,** two educators whom the Lord used to prepare me for *this season* of my life. They have now gone on to be with the Lord but the life lessons they taught are forever with me. It is my prayer and sincere hope that somehow and from some where in the eternal realms of glory they are able to see and rejoice in this day.

To my children **Dakisha** and **Trevon** and my precious, precious grandchildren. Thank you for sharing me with the world. It has not been easy but God has been faithful! May you enter into and experience *continual seasons* of stability, wholeness, wealth and prosperity*! I love you, always.*

To those that have *consistently* been in covenant with me throughout the years; **Prophetess Runette C. Jones, Apostle Leonard T. and Pamela Smith, Apostles Tyrone and Debra Giles and Prophetess Sonya and Deacon Leonard Fisher.** Your friendship, loyalty and commitment has been and still is invaluable to me. Thank you so much for loving me and coming to my rescue whenever I call. Thank you for discerning my heart and putting up with me, no matter how much I fuss! (*smile*) You all play vital and distinct roles in my life, from my personal prophet, my faithful rock, my general of intercession and my chicken spaghetti hideout! **I love you much!** *Smooches!*

To my **FAITH MENTOR** who taught me how to believe God for myself, *Prophetess Phyllis Morton.* I knew how to believe God for *everyone else* and see the manifestation occur in the lives of others but I did not know how to apply that same faith in *my* life.

Prophetess Morton you *"got up in my face"* and propelled me into *personal faith*! My love to you and your life-time companion, **Apostle Gary Morton** (Big Daddy), *Light Up For Jesus!*

To **Shepherd Mother Carla Alston** whom the Lord raised up in my time of need to be a succourer. You are my Phoebe, a true intercessor and spiritual warrior. *Thank you so much* for your untiring sacrifice, hospitality, generosity and labor of love! I know that your season has come! Enjoy it and all the benefits thereof!

To all my other friends, sons and daughters in the ministry, **THANK YOU** for your love, prayers and support. There are so many of you and I don't want to leave anyone out, you are <u>all</u> included. However, I would like to make special mention of the following: **Apostle Frank and Prophetess Sharlene Fullwood, Apostle Paul and Prophetess Ida Thornton, Pastor Vanessa Hayes, Bishop Vance L. and Pastor Vernell Dash, Apostle Bruce and Evangelist Patricia Lester, Prophetess Sharon Clark, Evangelist Helena Reid** *and my big sister who loves me much* **Derrian Bethea James!**

To **Rhema Prophetic Worship Ministries, Inc.**, *"Where the Proceeding Word of the Lord Goes Forth!,"* I cannot forget you! **Thank you** for loving, supporting, praying for and putting up with your Pastor! This is definitely **<u>YOUR</u>** season! So rise up and be *"a people of excellence doing great things for God!"* **Proton Believers! We Are *First!***

A *special dedication* to: **Apostle Jean and Bishop Thomas Porter.** Thank you so much for being there for me during a time in my personal and ministry life when I needed nurturing. Even though you may not have understood everything God was doing in my life, you did not become intimidated, insecure and shut me down. *Thank you for allowing me to heal and flourish.* You are loved and greatly appreciated. May you greatly increase, rise up, go forth and **WAM** the devil! *Smooches!*

Most of all, this book is dedicated to the one who gave it, **The Lord God through Jesus Christ by the power of the Holy Ghost! Thank you Father for EVERYTHING!** I especially thank you for revealing my purpose and plotting the course to my destiny! I love you with all my heart, soul and strength! **I am yours –** *forever.*

Contents

Introduction ix

Chapter One: Seasons
Anya M. Hall 11

Chapter Two: Spring
Runette C. Jones..21

Chapter Three: Summer
Debra T. Giles 27

Chapter Four: Fall
Leonard T. Smith 35

Chapter Five: The Winter Season
Paul Thornton...45

Chapter Six: Opportune Time
Anya M. Hall 55

Introduction

Many times we hear the phrase, *"it's your season,"* or *"wait for your season,"* without really knowing what a **season** is, how to identify it and how to properly respond to it. The purpose of this book is to empower you to walk in and benefit from the divine seasons of your life by identifying, defining and giving prophetic instructions for proper response. In order to do this, the seasons of the natural year are used as patterns to bring about spiritual revelation for your life.

I've asked some friends of mine to be contributing authors. They are anointed men and women of God, each with their own divine dynamics, who bring unique revelation to each season.

First, *Runette C. Jones*. Runette is a strong **Prophetess** and **Seer** of the Lord. She is used by God in a powerful way to reveal future events as well as speak the mind of God concerning His people. She brings to this book *prophetic voice* to those who find themselves in the **Spring Season**.

Secondly, *Debra T. Giles*. Debra is a powerful **Apostle** and **Spiritual Warrior** of the Lord used to mentor, train and release those called to the five-fold ministry. She brings in-depth revelation and instruction to those in the **Summer Season**.

Thirdly, *Leonard T. Smith*. Leonard is an anointed **Apostle** and **Visionary** used as a master builder and great oracle of the Lord. He brings profound reasoning and divine articulation to those in the **Fall Season**.

Fourth and Last, *Paul Thornton*. Paul is a dynamic **Apostle** and **Preacher** used as a refiner to the Body of Christ with emphasis on those in leadership. He brings admonition, clarity and structure to those found in the **Winter Season** of life.

It is my prayer that all who read this book will find clarity, understanding, direction and hope for every season of their life! May God impart spiritual revelation for practical application to those who seek His wisdom.

Chapter One

Seasons

SEASON – to sow, a sowing, a time of sowing.
SEASON – *an opportune and favorable time*
for specific events to occur.

"To Every Thing There Is A <u>Season</u>,
And A <u>Time</u> To Every <u>Purpose</u> Under The Heaven:"
Ecclesiates 3:1

Seasons are *recurrent* portions of time in which certain events will prosper if undertaken. The word recurrent is key in understanding how seasons work. First, it is important to note that seasons are a combination of the natural and the divine, the temporal and the eternal working together to provide a window of opportunity into the supernatural.

All things begin in the spirit realm which is called eternity. Eternity means endless. All things or beings destined for the physical realm must *pass through seasons* and manifest in time. Seasons are vital because they reveal purpose. Purpose is defined as the reason for existence, the goal toward which one strives and a determined course of action. Therefore, *seasons tell you what to do*

with your time and provide favorable conditions that empower you to accomplish your goal.

As mentioned before, seasons are recurrent which means that they repeat themselves. To recur also means *to bring again to one's attention or memory*. Thus, seasons are cycled to remind you of your purpose and give you another chance to accomplish your goal. Herein is the great love and mercy of God.

"For all have sinned, and come short of the glory of God;"
Romans 3:23

Sin is defined as **to miss the mark**, which implies *a determined course of action which failed to achieve its' goal*. This explains the above scripture. When God released us from eternity we were full of His purpose. Passage through the seasons of conception, gestation and birth empowered us to manifest in the continuum called time. Once in time, we were to take actions that would fulfill the reason we were sent here in the first place. This is found and clarified in the following scripture:

"Thy kingdom come.
Thy will be done in earth, as it is in heaven."
St. Matthew 6:10

We were sent to establish the government, rule and direction of God in the earth. This was to be achieved through the seasons or *sowing* of God. To sow means to scatter and plant seed for growing, to impregnate. We are the seed of God sown into the earth to bring about the will or purpose of God. The following scriptures will reveal this truth.

"Another parable put he forth unto them, saying,
The kingdom of heaven is likened unto a man which sowed
good seed in his field: But while men slept,
his enemy came and sowed tares among the wheat,
and went his way. But when the blade was sprung up, and
brought forth fruit, then appeared the tares also.

*So the servants of the householder came and said unto him, Sir,
didst not thou sow good seed in thy field? From whence then
hath it tares? He said unto them, an enemy hath done this.
The servants said unto him, wilt thou then that we go and gather
them up? But he said, Nay; lest while ye gather up the tares,
ye root up also the wheat with them. Let both grow together until
the harvest: and in the time of harvest I will say to the reapers,
gather ye together first the tares, and bind them in bundles to
burn them: but gather the wheat into my barn."*
St. Matthew 13:24 – 30

Jesus is speaking to his disciples using parabolic expressions or
stories to illustrate how the kingdom of heaven was to be *reproduced* in the earth through the kingdom of God. Now, this may
seem hard for you to understand and it seems as if the disciples also
needed an explanation.

*"Then Jesus sent the multitude away, and went into the house:
and his disciples came unto him, saying, Declare unto us
the parable of the tares of the field. He answered and said
unto them, He that soweth the good seed is the Son of man;
the field is the world; the good seed are the children of the
kingdom; but the tares are the children of the wicked one;
The enemy that sowed them is the devil; the harvest is the
end of the world; and the reapers are the angels. As therefore
the tares are gathered and burned in the fire; so shall it be
in the end of this world. The Son of man shall send forth his
angels, and they shall gather <u>out of his kingdom</u> all things
that offend, and them which do iniquity; And shall cast them
into a furnace of fire: there shall be wailing and gnashing
of teeth. Then shall the righteous shine forth as the sun in the
kingdom of their Father. Who hath ears to hear, let him hear."*
St. Matthew 13:36 – 43

Upon researching the previous scriptures it is found that
through Jesus Christ, the seed or children of God are *planted into
the worlds' systems* in order that they may be productive, repro-

duce and establish the kingdom of God in the earth. It is further revealed that the children of God lapsed into a state of unconsciousness in which they were no longer aware of their true identity and purpose. Satan, taking advantage of this, planted his wicked children in the worlds' systems as well. As a result, *the systems of the world are peopled by those both good and evil.* Jesus also states that things are to remain this way until the end of this specific age when the harvest or fulfillment of purpose has occurred. Then he will send his messengers to separate those that ensnare, cause to stumble, are fallen and have not kept the law of God's righteousness from those who have. It is interesting to note that at this stage Jesus is no longer referring to the world system as a field but states that it is *his* kingdom.

Remember that seasons are recurring among which is the definition to bring to one's attention or memory? God uses seasons to remind you that you have been divinely sown into one or more of the worlds' systems in order to establish his kingdom. While in these systems opportune, favorable times will occur for the success and accomplishment of godly purpose. That is why it is essential to **properly discern** or identify the seasons of your life!

To discern means *to determine the true value or nature of.* You must clearly identify the seasons of your life so that you will know what to do within them. This enables you to make the most of your time. Remember seasons come but they also go. You only have a specified period of time in which conditions are favorable to accomplish whatever it is you are to do in any given season. Therefore, the greatest heed must be given to which season you are in.

Many in the body of Christ miss season after season because they have allowed strong demonic **spirits of religion** to uproot them from the systems in which they have been planted. These ungodly spirits use the very **word of the kingdom** against the children of the kingdom. And because the children of the kingdom do not correctly interpret the Word of God, they do not rightly divide it. Thus, traditional religious leaders preach and teach that one should **come out** of the world. This is *not* biblical. Rather, the reverse is true. The following scripture reveals this truth.

*"I pray not that thou shouldest take them out of the world, but
that thou shouldest keep them from the evil. They are not of
the world, even as I am not of the world. Sanctify them
through thy truth: thy word is truth. As thou hast sent me
into the world, even so have I also sent them into the world.
And for their sakes I sanctify myself, that they also
might be sanctified through the truth. Neither
pray I for these alone, but for them also which
shall believe on me through their word;."*
St. John 17:15 – 20

These are the words of Jesus as he prayed to the Father for those disciples that were with him as well as those who were to come. He emphatically states that he has dispatched his disciples into the world and asks the Father to keep a watchful eye upon them to protect them from any hurt or injury which the devil would attempt to inflict upon them. He also states that neither he nor his disciples are of the world. The phrase *"of the world"* refers to **origin** and **source**. Thus, Jesus is saying that his disciples do not come from or derive their power from the world.

St. John 16:33b teaches us that in the world systems we will have pressure, persecution and trouble. Nevertheless, Jesus admonishes us to take courage because he has conquered, subdued and gotten the victory over the world and its' systems! Therefore, as long as we allow God to **continually sanctify** or cleanse us with the truth of His word, we will accomplish and prosper in the world system as we were meant to do all along. This is the season or sowing of the Lord.

Nevertheless, there are those who *still* miss their season in spite of all that Christ has done. **Matthew 13:3 – 9** relates another parable illustrating this truth.

*"And he spake many things unto them in parables,
saying, Behold, a sower went forth to sow;
And when he sowed, some seeds fell by the way side,
and the fowls came and devoured them up:
Some fell upon stony places, where they had not*

much earth: and forthwith they sprung up, because they
had no deepness of earth: and when the sun was up,
they were scorched; and because they had no root, they
withered away. And some fell among thorns;
and the thorns sprung up, and choked them:
But other fell into good ground, and brought forth fruit,
some an hundredfold, some sixtyfold,
some thirtyfold. Who hath ears to hear, let him hear."

After Jesus finished, the disciples asked him why he spoke to the general public in parables. He told them that the hidden secrets of the kingdom of heaven were only for those who listened to, accepted and adhered to His teachings. Disciples, children of the kingdom, sown into the world. In **Matthew 13: 18 – 23** he explains the parable.

"Hear ye therefore the parable of the sower.
When any one heareth the word of the kingdom,
and understandeth it not, then cometh the wicked one,
and catcheth away that which was sown in his heart.
This is he which received seed by the way side.
But he that received the seed into stony places,
the same is he that heareth the word,
and anon with joy receiveth it;
Yet hath he not root in himself, but dureth for a while:
for when tribulation or persecution ariseth because
of the word, by and by he is offended.
He also that received seed among the thorns is he that heareth
the word; and the care of this world, and the deceitfulness
of riches, choke the word and he become unfruitful.
But he that receive seed into the good ground is he that
heareth the word, and understandeth it;
which also beareth fruit, and bringeth forth,
some an hundredfold, some sixty, some thirty."

Notice the "eth" at the end of some of the words in the previous scripture. Whenever this suffix is attached to a word it means, *"to continue to."* Therefore, we find that many miss their season because they continually hear the message of the kingdom and continually fail to *properly interpret its' truth* and so, do not grasp its' significance. The enemy uses this opportunity to snatch the word away. Others hear the word and receive it superficially, never allowing it to penetrate their heart. These are they who have no stamina and give up, in and out during trouble and trial. Then there are those who are consumed with ambition, selfishness and greed. They never remember why they were sown into the earth and so do not produce the desired results. Only those who hear the word continually, correctly interpret and grasp its' significance will develop and produce that which they were sent to do.

Perhaps you've noticed that these last scriptures refer to the Word of God as seed that is to be sown into us. This is *still* the season or sowing of the Lord. Allow me to expostulate.

> *"Howbeit that was not first which is spiritual, but that*
> *which is natural; and afterward that which is spiritual."*
> **I Corinthians 15:46**

One of the things this scripture reveals is that natural things are a pattern or reflection of that which is spiritual. Therefore, the sowing of the children of the kingdom into the world system is God's way of *seasoning* the first or celestial earth. Seasoning is defined as to add flavor and interest to, to cause to become usable, competent and tempered, to make available and ready for use. This is the reason we've been sown into the earth.

> *"And the Lord God formed man of the <u>dust of the ground</u>,*
> *and breathed into his nostrils the breathe of life;*
> *and man became a living soul."*
> **Genesis 2:7**

In order to insure proper accessibility and production, a second sowing occurred. God sent Jesus Christ, who is the living word, to live in the hearts of those that receive Him. This is God's way of seasoning the second or terrestrial earth.

There is a third seasoning. It is the sowing of the new earth mentioned in **Revelation 21:1**. The word "new" in that scripture is *kainos* and means **fresh**. Fresh is defined as that which is pure and unspoiled. The reason this third sowing has not occurred is because it must be done with the seed produced from the previous ones.

Therefore, every season or sowing of God is a divine opportunity of empowerment when conditions are most favorable for the purpose of God to be fulfilled. That is why it is imperative for you to properly discern and take full advantage of your season.

In order to take full advantage of your season you must realize that *each season has within it the power to fulfill its' purpose*. No one has to round up the birds and take them south for winter. The power of the winter season activates the instinct to migrate. By the same token, no one has to pull the leaves from the trees in fall. No one tells the flowers to bloom in spring and in the summer no one paints red on apples that were green. **The power is in the season.**

Power is defined as *the capacity to act or perform effectively, the ability to do*. Thus, each season brings with it a supernatural power that gives you the ability to effectively accomplish that which God has purposed and ordained for your life!

Now that you understand what a season is, how it operates and why it is vital, the next question is how are you responding to the seasons in your life? Have you properly identified each season that has come your way? Or have you missed season after season for one reason or another? The message of this book is meant to help you through every season you may encounter in any area of your life.

Prophetess Runette C. Jones is a mega prophet in the Body of Christ. She is an anointed seer of the Lord with the mantle of the Prophet Samuel upon her life. Prophetess Jones was saved at an early age and was taken by her mother to sit under the ministries and tutelage of great men of God such as A. A. Allen, R.W. Shambach and H. Richard Hall. Prophetess Jones later attended Logos Bible College and is presently the Pastor and Founder of **Hazon Ministries Inc.** and **Hazon School of Instruction** in Ocala, Florida.

This awesome woman of God is greatly sought out by other leaders of the five – fold ministry for the powerful and accurate prophetic word in her mouth. An end-time runner, Prophetess Jones stands as a mighty oracle to the Body of Christ and the world at large.

Hear the prophetic word of the Lord as you encounter the seasons of life.

Prophetess / Pastor Runette C. Jones
P. O. Box 503
Ocala, Florida 34478
Phone: 352 – 208 - 6654
E-mail: hazonministries@wmconnect.com

Chapter Two

Spring

The earth is slightly tipped or tilted as it turns on its' axis. This tilting in relation to the rays of the sun causes seasons as the earth rotates on its' axis and revolves around the sun. Seasons are used to identify certain portions of time within a year. These periods of time are important because of specific happenings that do not occur during other parts of the year. The season we will prophetically explore is spring.

Spring. To appear or emerge suddenly, to move upward quickly, to burst forth, to shift position suddenly and to release from a restrained or inoperative state.

Spring is the season between winter and summer, a transitional state between two extremes. **Transition is the process of changing from one form, state, activity and place to another**. Form deals with shape and structure, state refers to condition and situation, activity speaks of function and performance while place deals with position and boundaries. Transition is a necessity.

The first day of spring is called the spring equinox. The equinox is a time when the length of the day and night are the same. This creates balance. **Balance** means to achieve a stable mental and emotional state. It also means to weigh as in to carefully evaluate. Another definition of balance is to cancel out all opposing forces. Thus, spring is a time when great deliberation takes place as to ones' state of being and function. It is a time of renewal, peace and serenity and most of all it is a time of planning and growth, which if attempted will prosper because all opposing forces have been neutralized.

The number of daylight hours increase in spring and most spring days have higher temperature than winter days. The increase in daylight hours has its' purpose.

"I must work the works of him that sent me, while it is day: the night cometh, when no man can work."
St. John 9:4

Work in this scripture means to toil and labor effectively. Therefore, spring is a season when one must hone their skills, increase in quality and expand productivity in order to bring about the desired results. This, no doubt, will require greater sacrifice of time, treasure and talent. However, it is necessary if one is to make the transition that spring demands. **Change is inevitable**. Spring is a time of change and transformation. Those who resist and rebel against change will never be balanced, productive citizens. The will of God for their lives will never be realized. They will never fulfill their destiny.

Spring temperatures are considerably warmer than those of winter and much cooler than those of summer. Thus, *spring is a season of comfort*. Comfort suggests ease, well being and relief. So, even though it is a season of much restructuring, re-evaluating and work, it is also a time when whatever one attempts to do will be *easy*. **It is a time of breakthrough!** Whatever has held the people of God captive must release them! They shall come forth suddenly! It is this sudden movement that will confound the enemy. Suddenly is defined as *immediate, unexpected* and *swift*. Many did not expect you to make it and those that did were not expecting it this soon! The enemy won't have a chance, by the time he realizes what is happening it will be too late! Sudden breakthrough! Sudden blessings! Sudden favor! Sudden movement! *Spring is the season of suddenlies!*

Nature awakes in spring. Flowers bloom and hibernating animals are aroused from winter sleep. It is a season when everything dormant is revitalized. **Dormancy is the condition of inactivity.** Things that are dormant have the *capability* of activity but are temporarily slowed down or suspended. Spring causes one to awake or become conscious, aware and alert. Lethargy and apathy are replaced by energetic excitement! The urge to produce is greatest in the spring. That's why it's called the season of lovers, for passions run high during this season of new life.

Passion is defined as a powerful emotion or appetite, strong desire and boundless enthusiasm. Spring infuses one with passion concerning their goals and dreams. Things they once thought could never happen now seem possible. They are no longer tired and drained but rise with new motivation to accomplish.

Therefore, one must fully know and understand seasonal change in ones' life. Spring is a favorable time for the Lord's migration. Migration means to move seasonally, to change location periodically, to move from one country or region and settle in another. Mammals migrate in order to birth their young. This says that sometimes in order to produce one must change location because where they are, conditions are not suitable for productivity.

Now hear and receive the prophetic voice of the Lord as He speaks in the earth concerning spring.

*"Even as the birds return in the spring so will things and loved ones return to you. A **spiritual migration** will come from the Lord and many will move to different areas for the purpose of God's fulfillment in their life. You know how he takes care of the birds of the air; just think how much more he loves you. Therefore, even as the birds find a place to nest when they migrate, so has the Lord already prepared a place for you. Even as this word goes forth into your life everything and everybody is in place. Those destined to assist you in achieving your purpose await you.*

As the trees grow new leaves and the flowers bloom, this is your season of renewal and revival. The gifts, talents and abilities within you that you thought were dead are now coming to life. The dreams that died along with your hope are now resurrected. The vision for success is ever before your eyes. You are reawakening as the Spirit of the Lord moves in the earth! The power of darkness is destroyed and your way is made easy as the Lord your God brings you into a good land! Even as specialized farmers raise crops or livestock that is suited for their region, even so must you properly discern the climate in which God has placed you so that you will know what to do. Operate in the anointing that God has placed in and upon your life and work the region to which you are assigned.

Do not despise small beginnings for the Lord has given you the power to subdue cities. Allow God to diversify His anointing in your life so that you will transcend cultural, gender and economic boundaries. Remember, the anointing that God is empowering you with during this season is one that causes you to burst forth, move upward quickly and increase in quality and quantity. Therefore, you must be sensitive and alert to receive instructions from the Lord. Know that the enemy that sought to stop you has been canceled! The times of struggle that you endured were just a test of your character and faith. From now on, while the spring season lasts, it's going to be easy. **I prophesy in the name of Jesus that it's going to be easy!**

The heavens now OPEN upon the ones who are in the spring season and releases power to produce! Power to accomplish! Increase and expansion manifest NOW in their lives! I command every receptive soul to SPRING FORTH! This is your season! Start or expand your business, invest, run for public office, go forth in ministry, build your family or whatever God has placed in your heart to do! Spring is the season and it's going to be easy!

*I speak to you now, **spring!***"

Apostle Debra Giles is a woman of God that excels in intercession and spiritual warfare. She is the Founder of *Deborah's Tree Prophetic School* where she mentors and trains those called to the office of Prophet as well as other five-fold ministry gifts. Strong in administration, Apostle Giles is used by God to bring structure, order and direction to the Body of Christ.

Apostle Debra is married to Apostle Tyrone Giles and together they serve as the Founders and Pastors of *Faith and Power Covenant Ministries International, Inc.*, of Durham, North Carolina.

The mother of four anointed young men, Apostle Giles uses her greatest gifts, wisdom, love and anointing to build her sons into godly men of integrity and power.

Apostle Debra T. Giles
P. O. Box 12164
Raleigh, North Carolina 27605
Phone: 919 – 683 - 1410
Web Site: www.faithandpower.org.

Chapter Three

Summer

"When his branch is yet tender, and putteth forth leaves,
ye know that summer is nigh:
So likewise ye, when ye shall see all these things,
know that it is near, even at the doors."
Matthew 24: 32b – 33

There are always indications to the entrance of a season. Leaves turning brown and falling from the trees signify the onset of fall as does the chilly temperature the start of winter. To the same extent the ripened crops and intense heat herald the arrival of summer.

Summer is the season between spring and winter and is one of the natural divisions of time used to temper the earth. We are earthen vessels full of great treasure and just as God uses natural seasons to balance the ecology, he uses the seasons of our life to develop character, maturity and harmony within us.

Several definitions of summer in the Hebrew include *hot, harvest, to gather, to sever attachments.* It comes from the root word **mowed** that means *an appointment, a fixed time or season.* This tells us that the summer seasons of our life are divine appointments. The purpose of those appointments are found in the definition of summer.

First of all, **summer is hot.** Hot is defined as possessing great heat, yielding much heat and having higher temperatures than is normal or desirable. Heat is a form of energy that can be transmitted by conduction, convection and radiation. When heat is conducted, something is used to transfer it from its' origin to the place of destination. When heat moves through the atmosphere of its' own accord it is called a convection, as in heat rises to the top. Radiation occurs when heat is emitted in the form of rays, as in light. Therefore, heat has its' purposes.

Heat is energy and energy is *power in action*. Thus, summer is a season of heightened power and activity. This power is conducted by the Spirit of God, conveyed by the Word of God and is meant to radiate within our lives.

Summer is a time of harvest that means to gather in that which is ripened and mature. In order to do this one must sever the crop or total yield of that which has been produced from whatever it is attached to. After which it must be brought into a place of sorting and inventory.

The intense heat and inconvenience of summer represent agitating and frustrating situations that cause you to mature. These situations can be caused by a variety of people, circumstances or things. An overbearing employer, a financial tragedy, an abusive relationship and so forth, can all add to your growth and development. What you produce as a result of this season is your crop.

After maturity, a crop must be severed from the thing that made it grow. This does not necessarily mean that the person or thing that caused you to grow is no longer a part of your life but that it no longer affects you in the same way. This is a time to take personal inventory of your life and become accountable for your actions and decisions. It is a time to separate from that or those who are not healthy or beneficial to your individual growth.

One of the crops harvested in this season is **summer wheat.** This is wheat that is sown in spring and matures in summer. In Matthew 13:24 – 25 and Matthew 13: 38 the wheat is likened unto the children of the kingdom which are the children of God. This tells us that the hot trials of the summer seasons in our lives are meant to bring us to fruition and maturity.

Sadly, most people miss the purpose of their summer season because of a condition known as **summer complaint**. This is a diarrheal disorder that occurs in summer caused by heat and indigestion. Having already discussed heat, we find that indigestion is the inability to break down and absorb that necessary for strength and nourishment. Diarrhea is a condition that causes looseness of the bowels. Therefore, many miss their season because they do not retain the wisdom and instruction they have received. But, rather, they criticize, grumble and find fault with everyone and everything else. The higher the temperature the hotter the trial. If, during this affliction the Word of God is not applied, murmuring and complaining will flow loosely, almost uncontrollably. For summer complaint we recommend this remedy.

"I will bless the Lord at all times:
his praise shall continually be in my mouth."
Psalms 34:1

Summer rash is another condition that can prevent the fulfillment of purpose. It is a rash caused by prickly heat during summer. This is great agitation due to the fieriness of trials in this period. Agitation comes to cause anxiety, protest and disturbance. It is designed to cause doubt and undermine your faith in God. The medical name for prickly heat is *miliaria* and is defined as a skin disease caused by inflammation of the sweat glands and characterized by small blisters, redness and a burning sensation. This is sure to bring about great irritability.

Thus, summer rash is a reflection of your disposition during your trial. You are inconvenienced, uncomfortable and annoyed. As a result you are overly sensitive, quick to snap at others, feeling helpless and angry. If you are going to make it through this season we suggest the following:

"My brethren, count it all joy when ye fall into divers temptations;
Knowing this, that the trying of your faith worketh patience."
James 1:2-3

If you do not allow the patience of God to work in your life you may find yourself the victim of heat related disorders. A disorder is an ailment that disturbs the normal physical and mental health of. Therefore, heat disorders not only render you physically unwilling or unable, but also affect your mind set or attitude toward. Two main heat disorders are heat exhaustion and heat stroke. **Heat exhaustion** is a reaction to excessive heat marked by prostration, weakness and collapse caused by dehydration.

Dehydration is caused by the lack of ingesting water. It is a dangerous and deadly condition for water is essential to life. St. John 7:38-39 speaks of the Holy Spirit as water, while Ephesians 5:26 typifies the Word of God as water. Thus, we are given to understand that we must be filled and empowered with the Holy Spirit as well as cleansed by the daily application of God's holy word. This will enable us to endure the summer season of life.

Heat stroke is another disorder and is a severe illness caused by exposure to excessively high temperatures and characterized by severe headaches, high fever with dry hot skin, excessively rapid heart beat and in serious cases collapse and coma.

Heat stroke is caused by exposure that implies that one is improperly covered. **Cover** is defined as *to place something upon or over in order to protect and conceal, to shield from harm, loss or danger, to protect from enemy attack by occupying a strategic position and to be responsible for defending.* Normal covering from heat stroke includes clothing, sun screen and shade. But for the summer season of our lives the covering must be greater. A godly Pastor and loving church family who consistently pray for you and to whom you are accountable makes an excellent covering. A group of trusted friends who hold you to your word is another. Loving family members with *pure motives* and your best interest in mind will always come to your defense. A wise and time - tested mentor who will tell you the truth whether you like it or not is another sure covering. Giving tithes, offerings and to the poor provides *financial covering* as well as establishing savings, good credit and sound investments. Like it or not, the bottom line is that we all *need* covering.

Because heat can cause more than health problems we must

acquaint ourselves with heat awareness. One of the functions of the National Weather Service is to inform the public of heat fluctuations so that they can properly prepare for it. These announcements are called heat advisories. A heat watch means that excessive heat is expected to develop within the next twenty four to thirty six hours. These are sudden, unexpected trials that are short lived but intense. Heat Advisory warnings mean that the daytime heat index will reach one hundred five degrees Fahrenheit for at least three hours and will not drop below eighty degrees at night. A heat warning is the same except that the daytime temperature is one hundred fifteen degrees. These are extended and sustained trails that must be overcome by longsuffering and patience.

Summer is long and hot and the further you progress into it the hotter it gets. Nevertheless, this sweltering heat has its' purpose. It brings those things that have budded to mature fruition. Fruition is the condition of *bearing fruit*. This tells us that the summer season is designed to develop character.

"But the fruit of the Spirit is love, joy, peace, longsuffering, gentleness, goodness, faith, meekness, temperance: against such there is no law."
Galations 5:22-23

Character is developed through adversity. Adversity means a state of hardship, affliction or misfortune. It is derived from the root word *adverse* that means antagonistic in design or effect, opposed to and contrary to one's interest or welfare. Therefore, the *fruit of the spirit* or godly character is developed during adverse situations and circumstances that occur in the summer season of life.

With this in mind it is not ironic to note that summer officially starts **hurricane** season. A hurricane is a severe tropical cyclone with winds exceeding seventy-four miles per hour. They originate in the tropical regions and usually involve heavy rains. They often move rapidly and in an erratic manner causing high winds, flooding, storm surges and high surf. This is a storm in life that brings a sense of being overwhelmed and helpless. It causes fear and confusion.

Most often people make bad decisions during this time because they panic and thus, are misdirected. Hurricanes are very dangerous because they combine violent winds, torrential rains and abnormally high waves and storm tides. Each of these individually can pose a serious threat but combined together they are capable of widespread destruction.

Violent winds speak of *strong demonic attack* and torrential rains represent *many problems* or much trouble. The high tides and surf are overwhelming, unrelenting situations that keep *battering away* at your faith. This is a summer storm. Another deadly summer storm is the **tornado**. Tornadoes are characterized by a rotating column of air that is funnel shaped and whirls destructively at speeds of up to three hundred miles per hour, pulling into it everything that is within its' path. These are *especially vicious* demonic spirits of gossip, lies, rumor and innuendo. Stay away from messy people and shady situations. This storm is designed to destroy or ruin you. Ruin means to render unfit for use. As in the natural when hurricanes or tornadoes strike, the advice is the same, take immediate <u>cover</u>!

As you can see summer has many challenges. Nevertheless, there is a time of relief and refreshing. **Summer winds** are gentle breezes released during the season. These represent brief periods of rest and reprieve in order to regain strength, focus and determination. Enjoy this time, relax and have fun. This period of summer nourishes you as a person by helping to develop inner strength and wholeness. It helps you to get in touch with your true self and gives you the courage to face hurts and wounds that have never healed. ***Summer winds bring the grace we need to persevere and survive.***

Because summer is a time of development, maturity and harvest, it is important that you produce. If your life has been unproductive, you may be a type of summer fallow. **Summer fallow** is uncropped land that is plowed during the summer season in order to pulverize the soil and kill the weeds. This prepares the ground for sowing so that it will produce in the next summer season. Your life is the soil and the weeds are bitterness, fear, anger, rebellion, unforgiveness, pain and every other negative thing you may be harboring as a result of traumatic events that occurred in your life. These things are preventing you from becoming a wholesome and productive person. They are building ungodly character traits within your personality. You must allow the light of God's word and his love to plow the field of your heart. He has so much more for you than an empty field.

"While the earth remaineth, seedtime and harvest, cold and heat, and summer and winter, and day and night shall not cease."
Genesis 8:22

This scripture reveals the methodology and principles that God uses to deal with the earth. Seasons of sowing and reaping, cold and heat, summer and winter are all extremes that can individually wreak havoc but collectively bring harmony, balance and the fulfillment of purpose. That is why it is so important for you to identify, embrace and respond properly to every season of your life. *Summer is essential to the divine development of God's promise within your life.* Without summer your heart would be cold and hard, your spirit would be dead and dry and you would be flighty and immature. You would have nothing to show for your life, no harvest, unproductive and fallow. Embrace the summer! Allow this season to bring forth the fruits of righteous labor and godly character on your job, in your home, your church and community! This is your season of achievement, accountability and maturation. Summer.

Apostle Leonard T. Smith is the Pastor and Founder of Fountain of Life Restoration Ministries, Inc. and LTS Global Ministries of Crystal River, Florida. He is an anointed Apostle of the Lord called to the body of Christ to raise up, equip, maximize and send forth strong apostolic and prophetic leaders who will bring glory to the kingdom of God in both the Christian and secular arena.

Apostle Smith was saved at the age of eighteen and has always had an awareness of the call of God that is upon his life. He is an anointed worshiper with dynamic preaching and revelatory teaching that impacts the minds of people everywhere. He holds a Bachelors Degree in Ministry from Logos Bible Institute and Graduate School of Jacksonville, Florida and is an ordained Bishop of the Rhema Fellowship of Churches.

The ministry and the anointing in the life of Apostle Leonard T. Smith is presently in great demand in the continental United States and Overseas. Your life will be transformed and renewed as you experience God through this anointed vessel.

Apostle Smith is the husband of Pastor Pamela Smith, the father of three and grandfather to two.

Apostle Leonard T. Smith
P. O. Box 2736
Crystal River, Florida 34423
Phone: 352 – 795 – 5775
E-mail: fountain@naturecoast.net

Chapter Four

Fall

"To everything there is a season, and a time to every
purpose under the heaven...."
Ecclesiastes 3:1

We are living in a day when all the church is declaring that we are in the right season, at the right time, with the right purpose without truly understanding the depth of what we are declaring. This word season in the Hebrew is **Zeman** and means appointed time or periods of time. In the Greek it is **Karios** which means that which time gives opportunity to do. So what we are actually saying is, that we have come to our time and place of opportunity. The appointed time is when something has been given a day or a date in which it is to bring forth.

When we look at **Genesis 17:21; 18:14**, God speaks to Abraham about the promise of a son and he uses two words as it relates to the time table of its' fulfillment. He uses "set-time" and "appointed-time." The *set-time* is when God declares or establishes His covenant and the *appointed time* is when he brings the promise into reality. So when we read **Ecclesiastes 3:1** it should read "To everything there is an appointed time."

One important principle of life that we must understand is that nothing just happens. For every action there is a cause, a reason, a purpose or intent. For anyone to live their lives based on coincidence and happenstance is to exist without purpose and reason.

"Before I formed thee in the belly I knew thee;
and before thou camest forth out of the womb I sanctified thee,
and ordained thee a Prophet unto the nations.."
Jeremiah 1: 5

To be ordained speaks to a demarcation, which means you are marked by God. Your mother had to meet your father because you were marked, your mother *had* to get pregnant even though the doctors told her it was medically impossible! Your parents might have divorced when she was in the second trimester of her pregnancy but you were already destined! Your mothers' tubes might have been tied but God untied them just to bring you forth! You were created for this season. You are not an incident, an accident nor a mishap, but you are the manifestation of a promise brought forth at the right time.

<u>The Power Is In The Season</u>

There is nothing that God created that reproduces outside of its' season. Anything that reproduces outside of its' season is considered perverse. To be perverse means to change the use of or to deviate from the right, true or regular course of order. Everything that God has created reproduces and brings forth in it season.

"And he shall be like a tree planted by the rivers of water,
that bringeth forth his fruit in his season"
Psalms 1:3

This is what the bible calls our due season when whatever has been planted is brought to its' full term and is ready to be delivered. No tree, vine or plant cast it's fruit before time. There are certain types of seafood that cannot be harvested out of season such as clams, oysters, and scallops. There is a certain time of year when men dress up in camouflage, clean and prepare their weapons load up their trucks and venture out into the woods with the expectation of finding game, this is called hunting season it is only legitimate when done in its' proper season.

When something comes forth it does so because it is the right season for it. Many people believe that if enough effort is put into an endeavor it will surely happen. While effort is important and nothing that is fruitful can exist with the absence of effort, it is not the key factor. Have you ever seen someone do something at which they were successful and you tried the same thing duplicating exactly what they did but to no avail? You ask yourself, "*why didn't it work for me?*" Because doing the right thing, the right way alone doesn't guarantee success, but doing the right thing, the right way in the *right season* works every time! That's why the attacks of the enemy are more aggressive in certain seasons than at other times because he's trying to keep you from responding properly in the right season.

> *"And let us not be weary in well doing: for in due season we shall reap, if we faint not."*
> **Galatians 6:9**

Due season is a time when that which has been in process comes to manifestation. Due is from the Greek word Idios which denotes one's own property or that which has relations to. In other words, the seed has to have a relationship with the season and the seed is subject to the season. So then it is *the season that places a demand on the seed* and prompts it and calls for it. As the seasons shift the seed begins to respond first the sprout, then the bud, then the blossom and then the fruit.

> *"Every man's work shall be made manifest: for the day (season) shall declare it, because it shall be revealed by fire;"*
> **I Corinthians 3:13a**

Everything that God gives to us, is in seed form and every seed sown into the earth is wrapped in time. Time is a measurable period in which an action or a condition exists and everything that is created in time has to manifest in the time that it governs. God who sits in eternity is the creator of time. He speaks into time and then determines the season when what he has spoken should come to pass. Everything in time regardless of what it is has to have a season or a cycle by which it is brought to maturity and manifestation. Anything that doesn't have a season or a cycle cannot reproduce. If a woman doesn't have a cycle then she can't have a baby naturally, and if a seed doesn't go through a process it cannot become fruit. Therefore it is the season that determines when time is to expire because everything in time has a day and a date of expiration. So, then, the power is not in seed nor is it in the time, but **the Power is in the Season!!**

<u>The Fall Season</u>

Fall is the time or season when the *external appearances* of things begin to change. This is how nature begins to prepare itself for increase and new growth. That's why the Word of God teaches us not to judge things based on the outer appearance, but to judge things based on the unseen, for things which are seen are temporal, but the things which are not seen are eternal. **(II Corinthians)** *Everything is not what it appears to be.* The season of fall looks like the ending of something but is actually the beginning of the process of transition that positions the earth for greater things. Whatever we see happening in the natural is a sign of activity already manifested in the spirit.

Fall is a time when we decrease and allow the Christ of God to increase the more within our lives. John the Baptist said, "He must increase, but I must decrease." **(John 3:30)** This is a time of gathering or bringing into position. Fall is also noted as a time of harvesting, but before there can be a harvest there has to be preparation. That is why God is bringing His church into alignment and is positioning her for the **Day of Manifestation.**

This season is also a time when the church begins to experience it's greatest opposition. I know for the church that I Pastor, Fountain of Life Restoration Ministries, as we entered into the Fall season we were confronted by much resistance from the enemy, not only spiritually, but economically, emotionally, physically, in relationships, and in marriages. Satan uses natural things to try and influence spiritual outcomes. I prayed and asked the Lord, "why have the attacks of the enemy intensified?" He spoke this in my spirit and said, *"whenever you begin to cross over into a new dimension, the winds will always become contrary because it is at this point of transition that the enemy tries to frustrate your faith and cause you to become weary."* Paul warns us in **Galatians 6:9** to guard ourselves against weariness because it alters our perception. We lose sight of our destiny and miss our season. Remember in the gospel of **Mark 6:45-48,** when Jesus commanded the disciples to get into the ship and go over to the other side, it was when they got in the middle of the sea that the storm arose and the winds became contrary. The storm is just an illusion, the enemy wants to kill you while in transition, to keep you from transforming and hinder your ability to birth forth.

The winds represent a shifting in the weather pattern as the temperatures begin to decrease. Everything in nature senses the shifting and moves with a sense of urgency to prepare for what's next. During this season animals gather food in preparation for the coming winter, those with fur often grow thicker coats, and many birds migrate toward the equator to escape the falling temperatures. We can learn so much about the timing of God just by observing nature, because nature responds to seasons and *the season determines the time* and the *time is a window of opportunity.* Remember in **St. Mark 11:13** when Jesus came to the fig tree expecting to receive it's fruit? He found nothing but leaves for the bible says that the time of figs was not yet. You can be in your season but you have to wait for your time. God is speaking to his church like never before and letting us know that we are *so close* to our time to bring forth. That is why we are experiencing pressure from the hand of the enemy. Nothing ever comes forth without pressure. God uses this pressure to form and shape us for the next dimension. If the baby is going to come forth then the woman has to push, and if the oil is going to flow from the olives, they must go through the press.

PROCESSING THE SEASON

Fall consists of three months, September, October and November. Each month holds significance for the fall season. Consider the following;

SEPTEMBER/TISHRI

September in the Hebrew is Tishri which is now the seventh month in the Jewish calendar. Seven is the number of *spiritual perfection* and the word seven means to be full or satisfied, to have enough. Jesus, when He had ascended into heaven according to the scriptures in **Ephesians 4: 8-14**, gave gifts unto men. These ascension gifts are called the five-fold ministry. It consists of the Apostle, Prophet, Evangelist, Pastor and Teacher for the purpose of bringing the church into a state of perfection.

September in the original Hebrew calendar is the Jewish New Year that ushers in the penitential season. During this time we see things happening that have great spiritual significance.

(1) The blowing of the shofar.
(2) The restoration of Kingship.

Here, God is reaffirming His vested authority that he has placed in the church.

"And I will give unto thee the keys of the kingdom of heaven: and whatsoever thou shalt bind on earth shall be bound in heaven: and whatsoever thou shalt loose on earth shall be loosed in heaven."
Matthew 16: 19

OCTOBER/MARCHESVAN (BUL)

October is a time during the fall season when the earth begins to experience an increase of demonic activity. Mainly because the earth is in transition and Satan is trying to manipulate the minds of men so that he is in a position to influence the course of the upcoming year. Look at the major events that take place during this month; **(1)** United States' fiscal year, **(2)** Halloween, which is a satanic counterfeit of All Saints Day. and **(3)** Yom Kippur a Jewish Holy Day which is The Day of Atonement. This is time when the church needs to repent and begin to purge itself from dead works because wherever there are areas of darkness Satan has a legal access.

NOVEMBER/ KISLEV

November is the last of the three months of the fall season, it is also the ninth month in the Hebrew calendar. Nine is the number of final things. This month signifies the end of the changing of the vegetation and the removal of the old because the earth is preparing itself for a new day. This is a time of shedding. Notice when the fruit begins to fall from the trees that the only thing to survive is the seed. This is symbolic to what God is doing in the church because he wants to bless us and bring us to our day of new things, but He can't bring in the new until there has been a removal of the old. This is why Paul writes in **Romans 8:19** ,

"For the earnest expectation of the creature waiteth
for the manifestation of the Sons of God."

<u>CONCLUSION</u>

As the season unfolds we understand that nature is able to discern its' seasons. In I Chronicles12:32 the bible compliments the sons of Issachar because they were men that had understanding of times, that Israel might know what to do. If nature is able to discern its' season then we who have been created after the image of God, should be able to discern the shifting and the moving of the hand of God.

In this season of fall we will experience God in three levels:

(1) **revelation,**
(2) **preparation** *and*
(3) **manifestation**.

This is a time of declaration and announcement when God is revealing His truths to His generals, namely the Apostles and the Prophets, to bring validation to the kingdom by setting the church in order. We have petitioned and cried out to God saying, *"Lord when shall you restore your glory and when shall we experience the latter glory?",* and God is saying to the church *"I cannot send my glory where there is no order."* That is why we have seen the resurgence of the Apostolic and the Prophetic office in the church. God is in the process of restoring, reshaping and reforming the present day church, bringing it into position so that when our Chronos time kisses our Kairos season we will possess the power to birth forth the promise. The window of opportunity is open, we must rise up and seize the season!

This is a season when we as the people of God must begin to move with aggression and not sit passively by waiting for something to happen. We are **proton believers**. First to act, first in motion not reacting but **initiating** the activity of the season. Fall is the season whereby we shed the old to make way for the new. *It is a season of death.* Death is defined as separation, thus fall is a time in which we separate from that which keeps us from progressing into newness. *Do not fear this season but rather embrace it.* Allow yourself to die to old mind sets and ways that keep you trapped in tradition and stuck in the quagmire of life. This is a season of release as you prepare to be reborn. This is your season. Fall.

Apostle Paul Thornton graduated from **Oral Roberts University** in Tulsa, Oklahoma in May 1988 with *dual degrees* in Management Information Systems and New Testament Theology. While attending ORU, he received his calling to the apostolic/prophetic ministry. In December 2000, he was **ordained** to the office of Apostle through the laying on of hands by the apostolic presbytery.

He is the founder and president of **Paul Thornton Ministries** located in Marietta, GA. His commission is to go where Jesus' light is dim and His voice is heard small. Apostle Paul's mandate from God is to *usher leaders into their rightful place in the Kingdom of God and help them fulfill their purpose and destiny in the earth.* God has placed a desire in his heart to train and build up, encourage and strengthen those in the five-fold ministry. Through the **Five-Fold Ministers' Fellowship** (FFMF) which he founded in January 2001, he pastors and fathers five-fold ministers and oversees their churches and outreach ministries. Providing spiritual oversight and training for those in leadership is the vision and goal of FFMF. Throughout the year, Apostle Paul conducts five-fold ministers' conferences, leadership workshops and seminars. The scope of FFMF is international in its' reach. Apostle Paul and his wife, Prophetess Ida Thornton, currently reside in Marietta, GA and have a daughter named Paula.

Paul Thornton Ministries, Inc.
P. O. Box 100
Smyrna, GA 30080
Phone: 770 – 422 – 8697
Fax: 770 – 422 – 6620
E-mail: apostle@ptministries.org
Website: www.ptministries.org

Chapter Five

The Winter Season

"The day is yours, the night also is yours;
you have prepared the light and the sun.
You have set all the borders of the earth;
you have made summer and winter."
Psalm 74:16-17

We see from scripture that *winter is ordained of God.* **Genesis 8:22** says that as long as the earth remains winter and summer shall not cease. Winter can be seen from two different perspectives. To some, winter is a relief from the hot summer weather. It is a time to relax and unwind from the business of summer. It is a time to hibernate. A time to remain inside doors close to family and friends. Many people look forward to the cold weather and the snow. For many, winter is the season to ski, snowboard or ice skate. It is a time to have fun and enjoy nature. For those who love winter, they embrace it as a season of change. For others, winter can be the loneliest, most depressing time of the year. Winter represents a time when things seem dead, cold and distant.

Winters are unpredictable because of the blizzards, storms and fluctuating temperatures. Nobody has a choice as to when the seasons come or in which order. But we do know that they are coming. Seasons come with regularity whether we are ready or not. As believers, we must be prepared for the seasons of change that constantly come in our lives. I believe that as long as we remain in our earthen vessels, winters and summers shall not cease. As seasons come, we must remember to embrace the changes and allow God to deal with us during each phase of life. I believe that *each season gives us the opportunity to grow and mature.* If we will allow God to deal with us according to His divine purpose, He will usher us into another level of anointing, grace and provision.

The one object in nature that must endure all four seasons is the tree. When the seeds are planted, it begins to grow and mature. While the tree is under development, it has no choice but to endure all four seasons. In spring time, the tree brings forth new leaves and fruit. In summer time, the tree continues to flourish and produce. In fall, the tree begins to shed its leaves. In winter, death and stillness seem to set in.

"Blessed is the man who walks not in the counsel of the ungodly,
nor stands in the path of sinners, nor sits in the seat of the scornful;
but his delight is in the law of the LORD,
And in His law he meditates
day and night. He shall be like a tree planted by the rivers of water
that brings forth its fruit in its season, whose leaf also
shall not wither; and whatever he does shall prosper."
Psalms 1:1-3

God sees us as trees that are destined to flourish. As we meditate in the Word of God continually, we are destined to be continual fruit producing trees that cannot be shaken! But in order to get to this place of fruition and prosperity, we must be willing to endure the winter season. **In truth, winter is much more than a season, it is a process!**

If we are to reach our destiny and purpose in Christ, we must go through it.

By the time winter arrives, everything has been stripped from the tree. There are no more leaves and fruit. Many times as the leaves are falling, branches break off as well. By the time winter arrives, the tree has become naked and exposed. What was covered up during the spring and summer seasons can no longer be hidden. There is no pretension...honesty is forced on the tree. The marks where branches have been pruned away or where disease has taken its toll can be clearly seen. Many times we walk around with smiles on our faces but inwardly we have issues that are hindering us from advancing in the Kingdom. **Winter exposes the truth that is in our hearts**. It is in the winter season that God puts us on the potter's wheel to fashion us after Himself. **Jeremiah 18:4** says,

"And the vessel that he made of clay
was marred in the hand of the potter:
so he made it again another vessel,
as seemed good to the potter to make it."

Whether we realize it or not, each of us have areas in our lives where we are marred. An abusive relationship, past hurts or rejections, unforgiveness and bitterness and not walking in love and longsuffering as we ought can leave scars. Whatever the reason may be, winter is the season that God chooses to put us on the potter's wheel. He exposes us for who we are so that we can repent and be prepared to bring forth fresh fruit in the next season.

Being on the potter's wheel is difficult on our flesh. Just as a tree can no longer hide the disease that is within its trunk, neither can we hide our frailties and faults. The potter now calls us into *accountability* through prayer and the Word. He looks at the clay and decides whether it is acceptable or not. The potter decides if he must start over and make another vessel. **Hebrews 4:12** says,

"For the word of God is quick, and powerful, and sharper than
any two edged sword, piercing even to the dividing asunder of
soul and spirit, and of the joints and marrow, and is a discerner
of the thoughts and intents of the heart."

As we are on the potter's wheel, God takes the Word and begins to judge us accordingly. **Our motives, actions and our hearts are**

judged. He looks into our lives and points out the areas of compla-
cency, compromise and sin. He gazes into the inner chambers of
our hearts to see if there are doors still shut to His presence. He
looks into the throne room of our hearts in order to see if He is still
occupying His rightful place as Lord. Throughout this process,
God is exposing our character, so that we can repent and mature.
His exposure reveals areas in our life where we should never be
complacent and comfortable such as the place we're in, our anointing, material possessions and our popularity or status quo. Winter
is the season where God pulls us aside for examination and takes us
to another level of maturity in the Kingdom. During the summer
we may have been flourishing and everything looked well in our
lives. Things could not be better! But God uses winter to shine His
light so that we can see where we are in Him.

*The winter season seems to bring death to everything that it
touches.* The trees seem to die, the grass no longer grows and the
days are much shorter. Although the tree seems to be dead during
the winter, it never stops growing. The growth is hidden from view,
deep under ground where nobody can see its development. **Matt
20:20-23** says,

> *"Then the mother of Zebedee's sons came to Jesus with
> her sons and, kneeling down, asked a favor of him.
> 'What is it you want?' he asked. She said,
> 'Grant that one of these two sons of mine may
> sit at your right and the other at your left in your
> kingdom.' 'You don't know what you are asking,'
> Jesus said to them. 'Can you drink the cup I am
> going to drink?' 'We can,' they answered. Jesus said
> to them, 'You will indeed drink from my cup,
> but to sit at my right or left is not for me to grant.
> These places belong to those for whom they
> have been prepared by my Father.'"*

The two sons of Zebedee wanted to sit in a place of anointing in
the Kingdom. They wanted to sit with the King of Kings. But in
order for them to do this, they would have to share in the same cup

that Jesus was about to partake. This was not a natural cup. Jesus was talking about a place of sorrow, persecution, loneliness, trials and tribulations. Those who are truly hungry for God and want more of His anointing and presence in their lives must be willing to partake of that cup. In order to be exalted and anointed in the Kingdom, we must be willing to die to our flesh...willing to go through the death process. It is in the winter season of our lives that God will ask us, *"Can you drink the cup?"* We must be willing to pay the price for the anointing that is placed upon our lives. It may seem like all is dead outwardly but God uses this time to deal with the inner man. It is during the winter season that God asks us to die to ourselves so that He can live through us. When God anoints us, He is authorizing and setting us apart for Kingdom work. The anointing empowers us to carry out His assignment for our lives. In order for the anointing to increase, we must decrease. When talking to the sons of Zebedee, Jesus had a full understanding of what it meant to partake of the cup. *Death for Jesus did not start on the cross.* Jesus partook of the cup on a daily basis. The religious leaders constantly attempted to kill him; He was rejected by his family, misunderstood by the disciples and His doctrine was challenged on every hand. He was called a heretic and a devil. Jesus paid a great price for us, not just on the cross but throughout his whole life on the way to the cross! Partaking of the cup was required for Jesus' resurrection. Death and resurrection were in the same cup. **God has fashioned winter to cause us to die to selfishness, wrong motives and carnality.** But he does not leave us there. If we will pass the test and go through the winter season, God will resurrect us to a new level of maturity and anointing!

I Samuel 16:1-13 talks about David being anointed King over Israel. David did not ask to be king. He was minding his own business taking care of the sheep when Samuel called for him. When he anointed David, it propelled him into a winter season. David didn't really have any real problems until he became anointed. Now he was a threat to Saul and he wanted him dead. He threw a spear at David on two occasions and missed each time. In another instance, Saul set him up to be on the front lines in the war against the Philistines so they would kill him but that plan failed. On another occasion, Saul sent messengers to David's house to kill him. By the time they got there, David was gone. Saul commanded Jonathan to bring David to him so that he could be killed but that did not work either. David was continuously on the run for his life. If we are going to be God's anointed, we must be willing to go through some suffering, trials and tribulations. While Saul was chasing David, God was working on his heart. In the midst of David's persecution, God was actually molding Himself a king. The same anointing that David was paying a price for, God was using to protect and preserve him from Saul. By the time Saul was done with David, his heart was totally surrendered to God. It was the winter season in David's life that fashioned him into a man after God's own heart.

Many of David's psalms reflect the sufferings he went through before he became king. Great loneliness, discouragement, depression and persecution were the valleys that David walked through. Many times he wanted to give up and die. At times heaven was silent and he wasn't sure God was with him. He doubted his calling. He didn't understand why he was going through so much with Saul. But it was David's determination and love for God that helped him weather the storms. It is in the tears, trials, and loneliness that God causes the anointing to come forth in our lives. The more we allow Him to deal with us during our winter season, the more we will see His anointing manifested in our lives. **Salvation is free but the anointing has a great price attached to it**. Many people want the blessings and anointing of God but they don't want to pay the price. If we are going to be used of God, we must be willing to die to self, the worldly system, personal wants, dreams and visions. Whether we like it or not, winter will come in all of our lives. When it does, we must decide whether to embrace the season and allow God to bring change. Or we can resist it through our actions and never enter into the destiny that God has ordained for us.

In the natural, there are preventive measures that can be taken to help trees gets through the winter season. I believe these same principles can be used to assist the believer.

1. **Prune the trees regularly**. Trees that are pruned on a regu-

lar basis are more resistant to storm damage by removing structurally weak branches. Constant pruning and inspection of the tree is necessary if it is going to remain alive and fruitful. **John 15:2-3** says, ***"Every branch in Me that does not bear fruit He takes away; and every branch that bears fruit He prunes, that it may bear more fruit."*** The purpose of pruning is to improve the quality and development of the tree. God's pruning keeps us growing and maturing. It hurts initially but it yields brokenness, humility and an increased sensitivity to the Spirit of God. If we do not allow God to prune us during the winter season, *bad fruit is produced* in spring time. No one is able to receive from us because the anointing in our lives has become stale and useless. When we go from winter season to winter season without pruning, we become exposed to the bad elements. The result is layers of bad wood develop. Where God wanted to deal with bitterness and unforgiveness, now He's also dealing with disobedience and rebellion. As the layers of issues increase, our hearts become hard and insensitive. It causes the death process in our lives to be extended.

2. **Beware of dead wood in the tree**. Trees that have dead wood are brittle and cannot bend in the wind like a living tree or branch. They are not resilient and do not "bounce back" or recover after major storms. Trees don't die over night. It is a process. When the wood becomes too exposed to the elements, the tree becomes sick and diseased. The disease spreads throughout the tree choking the very life out of it. *We as believers must be careful not to associate with anything that would cause death in our lives.* Sin causes death. Religion causes death. The traditions of men cause death. Anything that we love more than the Father causes death and it does not happen overnight. It too is a process. When we no longer are pliable or able to bend with the Holy Spirit's direction, death is setting in. Beware of idols that cause you to be disconnected from the presence of God. Then the wrong type of death occurs. Instead of dying to our

flesh, we're dying to His Spirit.

3. **Beware of cracks in the tree**. A crack is a deep split in the tree, which extends through the bark and into the wood. Cracks are indicators of potential branch or tree failure. *Unresolved issues in the life of a believer produce cracks.* Past hurts that are not dealt with produce cracks and open up the door to give the devil place to wreak havoc in our lives. While we are hurting, the enemy sows seeds of depression, doubt, fear and anxiety as well as tempts us to meditate on our bad situation. The end result is unforgiveness and bitterness. We must stay close to Jesus, our True Vine. We must stay close to the Source of Life. So that when these issues come forth in our lives, He can bring healing and wholeness. Cracks exposed to the winter elements can cause the tree to suffer needlessly. So let's allow the Holy Spirit to apply His healing balm on the cracks before the winter season comes.

4. **Beware of decaying trees**. Trees usually decay from the inside, forming a cavity. At the same time, new wood is added to the outside of the tree as it grows. The tree may look good on the outside but inwardly it is dying. **Matthew 23:27-28** says, *"Woe to you, scribes and Pharisees, hypocrites! For you are like whitewashed tombs which indeed appear beautiful outwardly, but inside are full of dead men's bones and all uncleanness. Even so you also outwardly appear righteous to men, but inside you are full of hypocrisy and lawlessness."* If there is decay in our lives, the Holy Spirit will manifest it during our winter season. We must make sure that the righteousness we are reflecting is not our own but His. We must be cautious concerning our motives and desires. Are we serving Jesus in order to build the Kingdom of God or are we looking to build our own kingdom? Does the righteousness that men see reflect the righteousness of the Kingdom of God? Even though this scripture refers to the religious leaders of Jesus' day, it is no different today. There are many people in the Body of Christ

that present themselves as if everything is well but inwardly their soul and spirit is full of *cavities* (unclean things). If decay is not dealt with, in time it will cause them to lose their soul. Beware of decay.

5. **Beware of root problems**. Trees with damaged roots will blow over in winter storms. **Matthew 13:20-21** says, ***"The one who received the seed that fell on rocky places is the man who hears the word and at once receives it with joy. But since he has no root, he lasts only a short time. When trouble or persecution comes because of the word, he quickly falls away."*** If we are to last the winter season with all of its challenges, our roots must be founded in the Word. Whether it is the written Word or prophetic Word that God has spoken to us, we must cling to it in order to get through the winter season of our lives. Winter comes with challenges and we must have something of substance to sustain us through the challenges. Christian television, radio and books are wonderful; but they do not have the substance you need to get you through the trials and persecutions of the winter storm. Cling to the Word, meditate in it. Only the Word of God will keep you rooted in the midst of a winter storm. A tree survives years of storms because its roots are firmly planted several feet below the surface. A tree that is planted by the rivers of water can survive anything that comes its way!

The reality of winter can be a real challenge for believers. It destroys every form of pride and arrogance. It often causes believers great discomfort and discouragement. Not every body makes it through the winter season. Because of the severity, some will turn their backs on God and decide not to serve Him. Winter is the time God uses to kill everything in us that is not like Him. I don't believe that God deals with everything in one winter season. We would not be able to handle it. So He pulls us aside on a regular basis and requires us to die again and again! We die so that He can live! Although a tree looks pretty dead in winter, it never stops growing. Though the tree is resting, its roots are pushing deeper. The growth is hidden from sight, deep under ground where nobody sees. The same happens in the life of a believer. *The winter season pushes us deeper into Christ and causes us to grow in areas where nobody can see.* We become anchored in Christ. God uses winter times to draw us to Himself, to establish His character, to anchor us in the resurrection life of Jesus and to strip us of fleshly lusts and desires that hinder the work of the Holy Spirit in our lives. Winter brings brokeness, humility and the life of God in the inner man. There can be no summer fruit without winter. The inner man is built up as the outer man dies. Remember this when the next winter comes your way. **Winter is a time for growth and maturity.** Do not fear or despise it...embrace it...understand it...bear with it...welcome it. Why? *Because winter comes from God.* Winter.

Chapter Six

Opportune Time

Anya Miller Hall

Opportune is defined as suited or right for a particular purpose, occurring at a time that is fitting or advantageous. Advantageous means affording benefit or gain, useful. **Seasons are opportune times.** The definition of time is a non-spatial continuum in which events occur in apparently irreversible succession from the past *through the present* to the future. In other words, time moves along a continuous line. That which has already occurred is call the past, the moment in which one lives is called the present and that which is to come is called the future. *Seasons bring empowerment that enables one to maximize the present moment.* It is that period of time, that window, when all things are favorable. The air seems to crackle with anticipation as destiny compels you to act. And act you must, the whole earth is groaning, waiting for you to manifest.

The word **manifest** means to show or demonstrate plainly, to reveal. You are a revelation within yourself. The word *revelation* has long carried with it a mystique. However, it simply means to unveil, uncover, and make known. Theologically it is defined as the manifestation of a divine will or truth. Therefore, a revelation is the uncovering of something that was always there but had not yet been discovered.

Friends, family, neighbors and co-workers are around you every day, year in and year out. Yet, no one seems to sense the growing seed of destiny within you. Sometimes you yourself are not aware of the greatness that lies within. The dreams and goals that seem so far fetched and unobtainable are evidence of the destiny within. You *must* identify your opportune time or season and take full advantage of it.

To take advantage means to make use of in order to progress, advance, benefit and succeed. **There can be no more missed seasons.** Rise up and take advantage of the season you are currently in. Learn, grow, mature, prosper and impact the world! Regardless of what the season may be, the truth of the matter is that *this is your season!*

Each season brings with it a purpose for your life which in turn releases you with purpose into the world. The purpose that you accomplish in the world releases seed into many lives and the cycle continues until the Kingdom of God is fully established in the earth. Therefore, *one missed* season can delay your destiny and that of the world.

How many seasons have you missed? What can be done about it?

> *"Daniel answered and said, Blessed be the name of God*
> *for ever and ever: for wisdom and might are his:*
> *And he changeth the times and the seasons:"*
> **Daniel 2:20 -21a**

God has the ability to alter the times and seasons of our life. This is because he operates out of eternity and so has the ability to dominate time. Anything that is trapped in time is dominated by it and subject to its' affects. Time *passes* and as such has an aging affect on anything bound within it. This is one of the reasons why discerning your season is of the most urgent, for even though seasons are recurring and will eventually come around again, you are continually passing through time. Thus, when your season resurfaces, the affect of time upon you may render you unable to take advantage of your opportune moment.

Thankfully we have a God who is able to *redeem* the time. He is willing to give you another chance. He operates outside of time and is unaffected by it. He is the master of time and with just a thought, the intent of his heart, he can bring you to your due season.

This leads us to another question? *What have you done to prepare for your season?* If indeed you believe that God is going to bring you into your season then you will have prepared for it. Lack of preparation is a sign of unbelief. Every mother who really believed she was pregnant began to prepare for the arrival of a child. They educated themselves, bought needed supplies, cleaned and decorated a designated place for the child and chose names. This is called *acting on what you believe* or faith.

Faith without works is dead and without faith it is impossible to please God. You *must have faith* to believe that God will bring you into your season and acting on that same faith you must prepare for what is to come.

It is not the will of God that your life be empty and meaningless. Each life is full of value and worth. The season or sowing of God is within you. Your opportune time or day of manifestation is near! Take full advantage, seize the day and maximize the moment! Remember, *every* season is *your* season. There is purpose, power and destiny embedded in it. Unlock it and use it to grow, progress and succeed! Impact the world! This is your *opportune* time.

A Prayer For All Seasons

Father God, in the name of Jesus, thank you so much for filling my life with purpose. I now know that I have greatness within me and that you use the seasons to develop and reveal that greatness. Please help me to properly identify each season of my life and respond correctly to it.

Encourage me during the long, hot *summers* of trial, testing, storm and maturation. Help me to embrace the growing pains as you develop your character within me. Give me the strength to break away and separate from those people, places and things that will keep me from the newness that you have for me. This is my *fall* season and shedding old skins and severing old ties can be painful.

And now to me, I cannot go through *winter* without your help. Lord, give me the grace and the fortitude to look inside of my self. Help me to confront and challenge the hurts, wounds, grudges, resentments, bitterness, unforgiveness and the anger. So much anger. Lord, please cast out the fear that has me bound! Fear of living, fear of loving, and of trusting all because I don't want to be hurt or disappointed again. Help me through the stripping of winter and help me to allow you to heal this tree that you may be glorified in the earth.

If I can get through winter, I know you will bring me into *spring*. This is a time of new life and new love. Please help me to harness my passions and remained focused as you suddenly release me into new positions of power and prosperity. I want to be fruitful in the earth.

Father God, I pray that your will be done in my life as you sow me into the world system. Help me to take advantage of my opportune time so that I will be prepared and function effectively.

This I pray to the only one who can redeem the time, in the name of Jesus, Amen.

Contact Information

You can contact Apostle Anya Hall by writing to:

TeKton Ministries Int'l, Inc.
P. O. Box 690786
Orlando, Florida 32869

Or

Email: tektonministries@yahoo.com

Or

Visit us on the World Wide Web

www.TektonMinistries.com

Other Books By
The Author*

Possessing the Gate! - $10.00
It's time to rise up and take dominion. Strategic instructions for possessing your inheritance! Learn what's fighting for and how to defeat the snake in the gate.

The Anointing of Myrhh - $10.00
Have you ever wondered why you must suffer? What purpose does it serve? Compare the lives of Queen Esther and the Apostle Peter to discover how suffering releases greatness in your life and moves you from levels to dimensions and ultimately to spheres of dominion.

Shadows, Types and Symbols - $12.00
This manual is for those who have dreams and see visions. Ever dream about snakes or that a big black dog was chasing you? Then this book will help you discover the meaning of your dream.

Behold, I Speak A Mystery! - $12.00
The divine mystery of lovemaking is revealed. Learn how God ordained lovemaking between husband and wife to mirror the inter-action of Christ with the church. Understand why Satan fights the intimacy between husband and wife. Defeat the enemy through the power of love!

Birds of Prey! - $10.00
God is calling for a new breed of warrior! Apostles and Prophets arise! This is your hour! Learn about different types of Apostles and Prophets that God is raising up in this hour! The hawks and eagles of the Lord are moving in strong and unique anointings to destroy the enemy!

Teach My Hands to War - $10.00
Learn basic principles of warfare based on Psalms 144:1. Find out the importance of blessing the Lord and discover three levels of weaponry.

Woman, Let Go of Those Secrets! - $5.00
It is a dangerous thing for women to hold on to secrets. Yet, they do because it gives them a sense of control. This book has a twist to it that you can't afford to miss! Women must let go of secrets so that all men might be free!

Stuck in the Middle - $7.00
Has God dealt with you to come out of whatever you're in? Having trouble? Can't seem to come all the way out? Are you stuck between bondage and deliverance? This book will help you come all the way out and reveal the consequences of those who don't.

To order books write to:

TeKton Ministries Int'l, Inc.
P. O. Box 690786
Orlando, Florida 32869

Send Check or Money Order made payable to:

TeKton Ministries Int'l, Inc. or TMI
Please include $1.50 for shipping and handling

<u>*You May Also Order via Internet*</u>:

www.TektonMinistries.com

<u>*Please allow 6 to 8 weeks for delivery*.</u>
Although we try to get merchandise out in the allotted time, there are times when circumstances do not allow us to do so. We request your patience in this matter. If for some reason your order is delayed, please contact us.

All listed books are self- published by the author.

<u>We'd Love to Hear From You!</u>
If this book has been a blessing to you in any way, please, let us know! Write or email us! Each contributing author's name and contact information is at the beginning of each section. If what they've ministered to you helped in any way, they'd love to hear about it. This will encourage them to go forth all the more! So contact us today! We'd love to praise God with you! This is your season!

<u>MESSAGES ON CD OR TAPE</u>

<u>Click on Edit</u>
Many with gifts and callings are ready to go out and be exposed on public platforms without proper preparation. They are not ready to be presented to the world at large. Click on edit will reveal the necessity of allowing a senior Pastor, Apostle or Mentor prepare you for public presentation.

<u>The Other Side of Through</u>
Have been going through so long that you've forgotten where it is you are going? Has "going through" become your permanent address? Well, there's another side to through and it's called out!

God wants to take you to the other side of through!

Maximum Capacity
God wants to take us to new dimensions. However, new dimensions require the ability to house a greater amount. The stretching that occurs may be painful but God is taking us to a place of maximum capacity!

Atmospheric Settings – *Apostolic Devotions*
A must have devotional tool that will usher you into the presence of the Lord and set the atmosphere for thanksgiving, praise, worship, and warfare!

All CDs are $12.00 and all Tapes are $5.00
Please include $1.50 for shipping and handling

SELF – QUESTIONNARE

1. Have I ever missed an important season in my life? _____
   _____

   If so, which one? _____

2. Why was that particular season so important in my life?
   _____
   _____
   _____

3. Has that season ever re-occurred? _____

4. What can I do to prepare for that season again? _____
   _____
   _____
   _____

5. What season am I in right now? _____

6. What should I be doing right now? _____

7. What is my purpose in the earth? _____

Use the lines below to journal your progress as you pass through the seasons of your life.

_____
_____
_____
_____
_____
_____
_____